Self Guidance

Lonzolia Lesure

First published by Dog Ear Publishing
4011 Vincennes Rd
Indianapolis, IN 46268
www.dogearpublishing.net

ISBN: 978-1-4575-3871-1

This book is printed on acid-free paper.

Printed in the United States of America

Introduction

These are my opinions for Life Guidance. My thoughts to mentor, encourage, and uplift those who are faced with life challenges.

Why It Is Important to Look Your Best

Putting thought into your appearance is one of the easiest ways to improve your social prospects and the way people see you. It falls under the broader category of nonverbal communication. Unless you're really likable as a person, a lot of people will have a hard time looking past a sloppy exterior. Looking better also gives you strong confidence in yourself.

How Do I Know I'm in Love

Real love, true love, is when your concern for somebody else's happiness, health, welfare, and safety is greater than your own.

Believe in Yourself

Don't listen to people who don't believe in your vision. Trust your decisions and love them. Tell yourself that you're great. Tell yourself you can make it. Tell yourself you will make it. Be you, have faith in your abilities, take on new challenges, dig deep within yourself to conquer fear, and never let anyone bring you down.

How to Talk to Your Child about Sex

Each time you successfully tackle a sensitive topic, the anxiety level (for both of you) goes down. If you avoid these talks, your child won't learn your values about sex but will develop his own from what he gleans from friends and the media.

Many adults feel awkward talking about sex with their children because they don't have much practice doing it and because they're afraid of telling too much once a discussion gets going. The best strategy is to try to answer questions calmly and succinctly, however unusual or embarrassing it seems. If talking about sex is difficult for you, try rehearsing your answers in advance, either alone or with your spouse or partner.

Why Do People Lie

Lots of reasons motivate people to tell lies. Even though each reason might be different, all of them stem from one cause, which is being unable to bear the consequences of telling the truth.

Lack of courage, lack of problem-solving skills, and lack of the ability to properly handle unexpected events may make escaping from a situation a much better option than facing it.

Consequently, lying is the result of being unable to face the results of honesty and of lacking proper values (having a tolerance for lying).

Never Force Things

Dont force things. Just give it your best and then let it be. If it's meant to be, don't hold yourself down. Just take your time, because when you force things, they don't work out the way they should. The best results come from full thought and patience.

Overspending

Overspending leads to low income and low level of assets. Also higher medical and miscellaneous expenses. Bankruptcy can be a serious result of overspending, so be reasonable and don't put yourself through stress that you don't need.

How to Sleep at Night

There are many ways to fall asleep, but here is one way you can do it if you don't have any in mind. Eat a light snack and then put the TV volume on low or turn it off, then get under the covers and relax and pray to God, then rest your eyes.

Dealing with Road Rage

Road rage is a growing problem on our highways and streets. Learning how to deal with road rage can help you sidestep the dangerous nightmare that often follows a road rage incident. You must realize that you can't control another driver's behavior, but you can control your own. When another driver cuts you off, how you react will determine what happens next. If you are able to back off, take a deep breath and remain calm. Then you can defuse a potentially violent situation.

How to Deal with Difficult People

Resist the urge to be defensive. Understand very clearly that you cannot beat these kinds of people; they're called "impossible" for a reason. In their minds, you are the source of all wrongdoing, and nothing you can say is going to make them consider your side of the story. Your opinion is of no consequence to them, because you are already guilty, no matter what.

Always remember to detach. When you're in the middle of a conflict with an impossible person, use the following strategy.

Detach. Staying calm in the heat of the moment is paramount to your personal preservation. Spitting angry words and reacting with extreme emotions such as crying will only stimulate the impossible person to be more difficult.

Disassociate. Remove yourself from the situation and treat it with indifference. Do not, under any circumstances, talk bad to the other person's face, because then you are stooping down to their level.

Being a Leader

A leader leads by example and is a hard worker doing what he or she believes in. A leader is also a strong giver and has love for God because God is the leader who makes all things possible. If God is in us, He makes us better people, leaders.

A leader has a vision. A leader sees a problem that needs to be fixed or a goal that needs to be achieved. It may be something that no one else sees or simply something that no one else wants to tackle. Whatever it is, it is the focus of the leader's attention, and the leader attacks it with a single-minded determination.

Embracing Moments

It's important to embrace moments, because moments you can't get back. The time you spend with people is what makes life. You learn to appreciate the moments more when you take your time, so embrace whatever you are doing, and embrace the moments.

How to Pray

Talk with God respectfully but openly. Talk with Him as your father. Jesus taught us to pray, "Our Father …". Recognize God as a loving father. Understand Jesus as a friend and a brother. Recognize the Holy Spirit as your comforter and guide. Come to the Father in Jesus' name. Begin your prayer with confession of your sins. In this way, the blood of Jesus cleanses us and prepares us to really relate to God.

Then when you're done, say amen.

Being Sad

When you're sad, it's important to keep God first in your life to ensure happiness, as well as to keep yourself occupied with things you love to do, and to keep positive people around you who will always cheer you up when you're down.

How to Give Respect

Being respectful is one of the most effective tools in building positive relationships with others, not to mention that it just makes people feel good. No one likes to be disrespected. Some people need more work than others when it comes to learning how to show respect. With a little time and work, showing respect can become a habit and a part of your lifestyle, rather than something you have to make an effort to do. Being kind and courteous comes into play here as a way to give respect.

Being a Man

A man is someone who's not afraid to admit his mistakes and not afraid to say I'm sorry if in the wrong. A man is someone who's not afraid to cry. A man is someone who will say "I love you" to a complete stranger, no matter woman or man and who has respect for others, especially women. Kind, courteous, driven, a man keeps God first in every decision he makes. A man is flexible and reliable at the same time. If necessary, he can start all over again at any given moment, no matter what happens (like if his house burned down). A real man accepts his fate and doesn't become a victim of it.

How to Stop Crime

We have hope to stop crime, but all we can do is reduce it, by setting examples with heart-filled speeches and doing more in our communities. Also by helping one another and sticking together, we can make change.

How to Deal with Illness

Living with a long-lasting health condition, also called a chronic illness, presents many challenges. Learning how to meet those challenges is a process; it doesn't happen right away.

Understanding more about your condition, and doing your part to manage it, can help you take health challenges in stride. Many people find that taking an active part in the care of a chronic health condition can help them feel stronger and better equipped to deal with lots of life's trials and tribulations.

Feeling Unwanted

If you feel unwanted, you should excuse yourself from wherever you are. Don't sit and take the tension, because you will begin to feel really small, embarrassed, and stressed. Just move around if you're not wanted.

How to Be Competitive

A competitive attitude can help you to feel energized, able to take on challenging tasks, and ready to achieve many things in life. Someone who's driven and is willing to go through whatever to make it, and someone who's willing to set the bar high—that's a competitor.

Being a Woman

A woman is patient and someone who takes pride in her appearance. She is full of confidence and is educated. She is happy with herself and her own abilities. She appreciates who she is as an individual, embraces her femininity, and is proud to be a woman. She is determined, driven, and able to accomplish great feats. Her ability to be strong is derived from her own knowledge, intuition, and ambition. A woman is a person who lives for God.

How to Deal with a Miscarriage

The best thing to do after a miscarriage is to keep God first and understand that everything happens for a reason. Know that God is not going to take us to what He can't take us through, so keep Him first and trust that He is going to help you move forward and carry you along the way. Stay strong.

The Approval of Others

If you are happy with the decisions you have made, then whose business is that but your own. Just think of how much you could achieve if you stopped letting other people's opinions dictate the way you live your life. Just know that you have your own mind and you, not anyone else, control what you are about to do.

Smoking

It's not good to smoke anything that's harmful to your body because your health is at risk and it's not good to put your body through so much abuse because you always end up paying for it—if not right away, then down the line, so treat your lungs and body with care. Don't smoke.

How to Achieve

You have to acknowledge your strengths and also identify any obstacles that may interfere with goal's achieved. Create a goal achievement action plan, then find ways to stay motivated and assess your progress. As you work towards achieving something in life, stop periodically to evaluate your progress. Use this as an opportunity to adjust your action plan if you're not moving quickly enough towards your goal or if you need to take steps to increase your motivation.

What Does "Having Your Cake and Eating It, Too" Mean?

"You can't have your cake and eat it too" is a figure of speech. It means you cannot both possess your cake and eat it. Once the cake is eaten, it is gone. The phrase can be used to say that one cannot or should not have or want more than one deserves or can handle, or that one cannot or should not try to have two incompatible things. The proverb's meaning is similar to the phrases "you can't have it both ways" and "you can't have the best of both worlds."

What Is Fear

Fear is "a distressing emotion aroused by impending danger, evil, pain, etc., whether the threat is real or imagined; the feeling or condition of being afraid."

How to Deal with Death

It takes time to get over something like death, and some people never fully feel the same again, but life goes on and you have to be strong. That doesn't mean that you forget about the person who has died, but you can't dwell on the death forever.

We must eventually get over a person's death, whether the person is a loved one or simply a church friend's relative you barely knew. The first step is to mourn. Let it all out. You also have to be there for others. Even if you are upset, you must remember that other people are upset too, so be there for each other.

How to Make a Decision

You shouldn't second-guess yourself when making a decision. Trust your decision and move on. Don't over–think,
because you will find yourself in a confused place and at
a standstill; so follow your gut feeling and proceed on.

How to Give People Humor

When you see a person down and always moping, you should bring them joy by making funny faces or doing something ridiculous to yourself so they can laugh. Let them know that life is short and they should feel happy to be alive because tomorrow is not promised, and we should live free and find humor.

Battling Drug Addiction

Having a drug addiction can make you feel as though there's no hope for getting better. But no matter how bad things have gotten, if you put your mind to it, you can beat your addiction. Start by defining your reasons for quitting, since that will help you stay strong throughout the process. Then make a good plan and draw on help from support groups and counselors as you deal with withdrawal and start creating a life without drugs.

What Is a Power Move

You need guts to make power moves because they will be scary, they will make you uncomfortable, and they will make you fearful. To overcome all of these negative traits, you need balls. Power moves are the foundation for success, for fast success—not overnight success, but success in five to ten years.

If you can continue to make power move after power move, you will increase your chances of finishing at the top of the top. Remember to keep God first while making power moves. He is the key to making these things happen.

Why Is Health Important

There are several benefits of a healthy life. Your body becomes free from various forms of disorders and thus, you get a longer life. You can live a life without suffering from any aches, pain, or discomfort. In every sphere of your life, you will be able to perform to the best of your ability. Doing excellent work helps you to be a valuable member of a healthy society. Besides, when you are physically fit, it is reflected on your face, so you look attractive and start feeling good about yourself! If you have a fit body, you can lead a physically active life even after growing old. This is because the body can heal the regular wear and tear associated with aging faster. In short, health and wellness bring about a drastic improvement in the overall quality of your life.

What Is Voting

Your vote is your voice as an American citizen. It's your opportunity to be heard, to hold elected officials accountable for their decisions, and to have a say in important issues that affect your community. Your vote makes a difference.

Caring

It's very important to care about others because there are very few who do. Kindness and strong love will bring good energy and positive people. It's also good to do good things unexpectedly for others. That's a good way to show you care, so let's do more and say more caring things so we can form more caring people.

Having Friends

It's cool to have friends if they support your vision and give you advice. Friends stick with you through whatever you're going through in life. They are trustworthy, loyal, truthful, honorable, and people who will be themselves and not someone else just to please you.

Why Should We Live

Sometimes we live life by what we see, and sometimes that takes a toll on us and makes us depressed and out of sync. We also sometimes begin to let life take a hold of us instead of us taking a hold of it. We should live because God put us here to serve him. Remember this when you feel like life is too much and you feel like giving up.

How to Act in an Interview

Walk straight with your head held high, and stand until you are asked to sit down. Smile and give a firm handshake to each person in the room. Remember that your body language tells the interviewer about you, so maintain direct eye contact throughout the interview. Instead of folding your arms across your chest, place them casually on your lap. This makes you look confident. To avoid looking nervous, do not use gestures or fidget while speaking. Speak in a soft but audible voice throughout the interview, and always look presentable. Appearance is everything, so dress your best.

Dealing with Abuse

Emotional abuse comes in many forms. Sometimes, it's years' worth of a boyfriend or girlfriend, husband or wife wearing you down; sometimes, it's a romantic entanglement that takes a turn into this dangerous territory. It can even come in school under a dominating teacher or at work under a bad boss. Whatever abuse you have suffered, you can begin to overcome by moving around and keeping God first and asking Him to guide you.

Sometimes people who have experienced abuse get advice—from others or from their own internal voice—to just "move on," "forget the past," or "let go" of negative memories. Such advice may be well-intentioned (although, if it comes from the abuser, it may be self-serving), but it is not easy to accomplish and may not be healthful or helpful at first. Letting go and practicing forgiveness can be helpful goals for a survivor of abuse, dealing first with feelings of anger, grief, guilt, and other painful emotions resulting from the abuse is likely necessary before trying to "move on."

How to Start a Career

If you take time at the beginning to discover what you really want to do in your work life, you can then explore possibilities and move forward. Remember to keep God first, and He will help you as you begin to put one foot forward. Stay driven, keep your goal in sight, work hard, and shoot for the stars.

Feeling Lost

Sometimes we feel lost because we don't have God in our lives, and that's who we need when moving forward. Feeling lost is also a part of confusion, so keep your eye on what's important and on what drives you, because without God and with no drive, you will always feel lost and confused.

Feel lost no more. The devil is the main cause of destruction. Keep plugging away, and don't let him win.

Feeling Like Giving Up

It's easier to drive off the road than to stay on it, meaning it's easier to give up than to stay focused, but stay strong and overcome life's distractions.

The devil's always busy—don't let him pull you down and confuse you. Keep God first—He will keep you protected and will give you the energy to stay positive and not give up.

Why Is Education Important

Education is important because we all need it to function in life. Also in the future its going to be about two important things revenue and knowledge. So just keep that in mind. Also, it's better to know something than to not know, especially when someone asks you a question, so don't be afraid to learn new things. Education is key.

Why Do People Hoard

There are complex reasons behind hoarding. Below are some examples.

- A parent who has lost a lot in life may feel compelled to hang on to things out of fear of future loss--the loss may have been a job, family members, family structure, a house, items, etc.

- A parent who is suffering from depression, anxiety, or a mental illness may derive comfort from hanging on to things. Initially, the items hoarded may carry some meaning that gets lost over time, but the hoarding instinct remains.

- Sometimes a parent may be trying to create a sense of stability during difficult times, such as when moving around a lot or job hopping, and stuff makes up the gap in between the uncertainty of life in general and the certainty of things.

Being Adventurous

The best way to find new adventures is through new people. Everybody has different experiences and different backgrounds; every person can teach you something new. Maybe that guy sitting across from you at the coffee shop can show you how to climb a mountain, maybe even teach you how to fish.

Always be on the lookout for new things to do. Read the local papers, and ask people. Go to a local farm and ask if you can milk a cow, film a documentary, meditate with Buddhist monks. Whatever it is approach it with an open mind and a good attitude, and thank people for giving you the opportunity for trying something new.

Dealing with Regret

Use your regret as a learning tool. Use the opportunity to become better at adapting, then strengthen your ability to focus on things you can control. You have to get better at accepting blame to change your way of thinking.

The Past

Stop living in the past! There is virtually nothing you can gain by wallowing in mistakes you have previously made. Take past mistakes as lessons learned, and move forward. You cannot wholeheartedly move on to a better future if you are constantly looking behind you. Let the past be the past.

Free Will

To believe in free will is to believe that human beings can be the authors of their own actions and to reject the idea that human actions are determined by external conditions or fate. We are in control of what we do on earth but never take advantage of free will.

Keeping Your Enemies Close

You have to keep your friends close and your enemies closer because that way, you will know their every move and you will be aware of what's going to happen before it does.

How to Stay Humble

Humble people do not rub their skills in people's faces. Do not mention what you're good at, because others will. Humility comes from someone who doesn't glorify him- or herself when asked a question. Someone who doesn't toot their horn stays humble.

CPSIA information can be obtained
at www.ICGtesting.com
Printed in the USA
LVOW13s0327140218
566498LV00008B/82/P